The
SECRETS
OF A SUCCESSFUL CHRISTIAN MARRIAGE

BY

Emeka Divine

The Secrets of a successful Christian marriage.

Copyright © 2021 Emeka Divine

All rights reserved. No portion of this book may be reproduced in any form without permission from the publisher, except as permitted by U.S.

Copyright law. For permission contact:
divinenationd@gmail.com

Table of content

Introduction.

Chapter One

Marriage is a covenant.

Chapter Two

There is a vision behind every successful marriage.

Chapter Three.

There's a best time to marry.

Chapter Four

Acquaint yourself with knowledge.

Chapter Five

Know what you want.

Chapter Six

Success in Marriage.

Chapter Seven

Pillars of success in marriage.

Conclusion

Introduction

In today's world, many people including Christians don't understand the context of marriage, and what marriage means from biblical perspective. It is not the popularly known word called WEDDING, marriage is deeper than that, I consider wedding as a door to the world of marriage. It is what commissions marriage.

We have seen a lot of abuses been made out of marriages just because the meaning and the understanding has been overlooked.

God almighty designed marriage to be a solemn covenant between a man and a woman. It was intended by God to bring mutual joy fulfilment and for the help and comfort of one another.

Today people view Marriage as a social relationship that can be entered into and severed at will. This is clearly seen by the manner in which some people uncertainly enter into marriage and how quickly they get out of it.

Marriage is not something humans came up with – it was instituted by God according to **Genesis 2:22-25** and **Ephesians 5:22-33**

Let's come to the understanding of why God created marriage. **In genesis 2:18 God said it is not good for a man to be alone; I will make him a help meet for him**.

First, God created marriage for your completion - to fill in gaps!

God saw the need, and he created the solution, in other words, he filled the gap.

Secondly, God created marriage for man to obtain favor. As was seen in **proverb 18:22 whosoever finds a wife finds a good thing, and obtains favor from him.**

Just like in the natural, if you want to obtain favor from someone you must know what to do. In the same way God designed marriage as a means of obtaining favor from him.

Thirdly, God designed it for emotional satisfaction as seen in **proverb 5:19 let her be as the loving hind and pleasant roe; let her breasts satisfy thee at all times; and be thou ravished always with her love.**

Fourthly, God designed it for higher functionality and efficiency. As seen in **Ecclesiastes 4:9 two are better than one, because they have good reward for their labor.**

So, we have seen that marriage is eternal! This mystery is profound. marriage is 60% spiritual because God that formed it is a spirit.

It is not what one should enter into unconsciously, it is what you should enter into it well acquainted with knowledge.

There are a lot of things anyone going into marriage should be aware of first, spiritually and secondly, physically, and must be willing to do them if one desires a blissful marriage.

Now, let's study marriage and how to make it a success because that's God's purpose for creating marriage.

Chapter One

Marriage is a covenant.

We know that there is nothing more important to God than covenant.

When you marry, you have entered into the covenant of marriage, you are not just tying your life to your spouse and children but also to God. Your words, behaviors, attitudes and lifestyle entirely should reflect the fact that covenant marriage touches God's heart.

When a man takes a woman to the altar to wed, God bears witness, as we see in **Malachi 2:14-16 … because the LORD was witness between you and the wife of your youth,"** and when this is done that marriage has involved God and you know, God is a covenant keeping God according **Deuteronomy 7: 9** which says, **"know therefore that the lord thy God, he is God, the faithful God, which keeps covenant and mercy them that love him and keeps his commandment to a thousand generations."**

It is important for Christians to understand that marriage is a covenant relationship that involves not just the couples but God also.

From **Malachi 2:14**, we can see that God is the first witness in marriage. In **Genesis 2:18** where God brought the woman Eve to the man Adam, stating that, it is not good for a man to be alone. We can understand that marriage is divine!

Marriage was not created as a mere romantic relationship but a way of modeling God's covenant keeping nature. Indeed, it's all over scriptures that God is very passionate about the sanctity, and stability of the home. That's why he has set some verses to ensure that every home at is peace and successful.

You want to know how passionate God is about marriage?

In **John 2:1-11**, Jesus Christ attended a wedding ceremony, and first miracle that he performed was at that wedding.

Therefore, it is clear from the word of God that marriage is patterned after God's relationship with the church **Ephesians** 5:32-33, which is loving, faithful, and everlasting.

Marriage is a sacred institution; it is very important for every Christian in particular to understand this fact.

Many marriages will be better if the husband and the wife understand it as a covenant.

But what is Marriage?

Going through the word of God it is very clear that marriage is a union, the coming together of two people of opposite sex with a view to building a God centered home.

Marriage is a unique covenant relationship ordained by God for a man and a woman to first give, and secondly to receive satisfaction of their healthy needs and desires.

But what is a *covenant*?

A covenant is an oath-bound relationship between two parties. A chosen relationship in which two parties make binding promises to each other.

The "word" covenant, is actually of Latin origin, convenire. Meaning a coming together. A formal contractual agreement between two people or more parties with each party agrees to do something as a prerequisite to receiving some benefits.

human bond that holds all of God's work on the planet together.

It is important to have a great understanding of this. Whether you are single or you're married.

But what makes marriage a covenant relationship.

Let us look at factors:

- **It brings to lives together to form one.**

According to **Mark 10:7-8** they are not more twin but one flesh, not just one spirit but one flesh.

This is very critical. Just as accepting Jesus Christ as your Lord and personal savior brings you into a covenant relationship and union with God. In the same way, the husband and wife is joined and seen one before God when they get married. This very clear from the word of God.

When your lives are truly joined, you will help each other in every possible way to attain higher levels, spiritually, mentally, physically.

Therefore, husband and wife, don't do to your spouse what you will not tolerate. The two shall become one flesh (**mark 10:8**) therefore whatever good thing you desire for yourself, should be desired for your spouse.

Treat your spouse the way you want to be treated. Husband and wife ensure you do to each other only what you want to be done to you, it is very important.

- **It is written and bound by oath**

Habakkuk 2:2 God said write the vision and make it plain upon the tables.

The covenant of marriage is called, when it's documented and sealed by an oath. Whether by authorized church license or in government declaration of marriage.

In **Exodus 20** God listed the terms of his covenant with the Israelites, in **Exodus 34:7** when God made his covenant with Israel, he commanded Moses to write it down. Similarly, the marriage certificate serves as a document that binds both the husband and the wife in marriage.

- **There're witness to it.**

In **Malachi 2:14** God originated marriage and he is the principal witness to your marriage. Of course, there are usually other witnesses. Such as parents, family, friends and so on. Which stand as cloud of witnesses.

In the word of God, you see how this is clearly stated. In **Gen 29:22** when Jacob was a kind of deceived in marriage after he had served Laban for seven years; all the men gathered. When Boaz was to take Ruth as wife, he called his Kings men to bear witness to the union **Ruth 4.**

If God is the principal witness, then you need a personal relationship with him.

Success in marriage is a triangular. On one side you have the man, on the other side, you have the woman and at the edge, you have God.

It is a three-fold cord that cannot be easily broken.

The closer you get to God, the closer you get to your spouse. This is very important. Your strong relationship with God enables you to keep your part to your partner. Your stand with God will show in how you treat your spouse so let your attitude towards your spouse shows that you genuinely love and reference God in your relationship.

- **It has a token.**

Every covenant has a token. When God entered a covenant with Noah, he gave him a token. Which is the rainbow **Genesis 9:16** today rainbow is still in the sky as a part of that covenant.

Jesus Christ is a token of God's love covenant with man **John 3:16**

There is usually a token in every covenant. In the same way in marriage, the exchange of rings between the husband and the wife is a token of this covenant.

Many people exchange rings, but they don't know the meaning. We hear declaration at wedding such as," I *give you this as a token of my love for you.*

- **There is a change of name**.

Abraham's name was changed as result of the covenant God had with him **Genesis 17:5.** Jacob was changed to Israel after the covenant God had with him **Genesis 32:28**

- **A meal is shared.**

when a covenant is called a meal is shared. In **Genesis 31:51-54**

What is termed as the Lord's supper is the unveiling of the new covenant **1 Corinthians 11**, this validates why the communion is being taken at weddings and there's an exchange of meal which is known as their first meal together. This is symbolic.

It is bond God has ordained for a lifetime, **Mark 10:9**

The marriage covenant is a lifetime commitment, only death should bring you apart. the scripture is very clear about this **1 Corinthians 7:39** the vows made during weddings also validates this.

Therefore, devoice, separation was not designed to be part of the covenant.

When a man and a woman get married, a lineage is a made and generations are connected to them.

Terms and conditions that must be obeyed in this covenant.

The Bible is a raw material you need for your success in marriage. Dig into it, study it and put it to work.

- Husband and wife must fulfill their part of the covenant if they must enjoy the best that marriage offers.

- Husband you have a covenant responsibility to love your wife as Christ loves the church. Wife

- Wife you have a covenant responsibility to submit to your own husband as unto the Lord **Ephesians 5:22**

Husband and wife also, have roles to play, for instance, you the husband provide leadership and make physical, spiritual and material provision for your family.

You must provide as a husband. This is one of the major challenges in homes.

Wife you have a covenant responsibility too, to support and help your husband in every way possible.

- You also have to be faithful to your spouse as part of the covenant this is clearly stated in the Bible, **Hebrews 13:4**

Your marriage is at the mercy of what you make out of it. So, take steps, don't wait for things to just get better, successful marriage is action oriented.

Chapter Two.

There's a best time to marry.

There's a Best time to be married, there is a best time to start a home, there's a best time to start a family!

In **Ecclesiastes 3:1.** To everything there is a season, and a time to every purpose under the heaven.

In verse **Ecclesiastes 3:3** the later part of it says **...and a time to build up. Yes, there's a time to build up.**

Now, let's look at Biblical way to build anything that must be successful. In **Luke 14:28-30** Jesus said, **"for which of you, intending to build a tower, sits not down first, and counts the cost, whether he have sufficient to finish it?**

29 Lest haply, after he hath laid the foundation, and is not able to finish it, all that behold it begin to mock him,

30 saying, this man began to build, and was not able to finish.

Marriage like anything else requires preparation. Many people spend years studying a course in school, but they don't spend time preparing for marriage. They think, all you need to make a successful marriage is money. That's not true! I believe you must have seen wealthy people whom their marriage crashed! That's because there's something bigger than money that is required. And that's knowledge. Biblical knowledge.

But what is the best time to marry?

The following factors will tell you the best time to marry:

- **When you have discovered your purpose or your assignment**.

This is really vital for men especially, in the first marriage in **Genesis 2:22** which says, **"then the LORD God made a woman from the rib he had taken out of the man, and he brought her to the man**. Before God did that, he first gave Adam a task. In **Genesis 2:15, The LORD God took the man and put him in the Garden of Eden to work it and take care of it.**

Adam had a work! Before you consider getting married as a man you must have a work – a means of sustenance. Likewise, women if a man ask for your hand in marriage try to find out if he has something doing – a work that can sustain and take care of marital responsibility.

Now, that the man Adam, had work. That was when God brought a helper to him. **Genesis 2:18 The LORD God said, "It is not good for the man to be alone. I will make a helper suitable for him."**

God made a woman to be a man's helper. Simply put it this way, her man's help meet.

You see why you must have something doing!

That is also vital because a man has a great responsibility of providing for the upkeep of the home **1 timothy 5:8**

But if anyone does not provide for his own, and especially for those of his household, he has denied the faith and is worse than an unbeliever. Take note of this fact!

Chapter Three

There is a vision behind every successful marriage.

I would like to let you know that success in marriage starts with a vision. In **Genesis 11:6,** hear what God said about these people **...and now nothing will be restrained from them, which they have imagined to do.**

Every action originates from vision. In other words, just as God told Abraham "**I am giving all this land, as far as you can see... Success in**

marriage is largely dependent on as far good as your eyes can see.

Gen13:15

Vision gives birth to goals. It is when you have seen it that you will be able to work towards it.

So just before you say to

yourself, I am ready. You have to answer this question to yourself. What kind of Godly home do I desire?

It is very vital just before you start your marital quest. and in case you're already married, it's not still late to get things right again.

Here's what the Bible said in **Job22:2**

You will decide on a matter, and it will be established for you, and light will shine on your ways.

So, you must deliberately decide on whether you want a successful marriage or not.

Chapter Four

Acquaint yourself with knowledge.

I would like to say this, successful marriage is not a Gift you will stumble into immediately you got married. Despite how peaceful, blessed and satisfying God wants marriages to be, he can't help it when spouses are ignorant.

Here is what God said about knowledge to show you how important it is for us. **Hosea 4:6** my people are destroyed from lack of knowledge. "Because you have rejected knowledge, I also reject you as my priests, because you have ignored the law of your God...

In **Mathew 19:4** an issue of marriage was raised and here is what Jesus said

"**And he answered and said unto them, have you not read...** So, God expects you to be well acquainted with scriptural facts before you go into it.

Also, in **1 peter 3:7** the Bible said,

Likewise, ye husbands, dwell with them according to knowledge, giving honor unto the wife, as unto the weaker vessel, and as being heirs together of the grace of life; that your prayers be not hindered.

Marriage can't be successful without knowledge, and it's not a once and for all event, you must keep seeking for knowledge even in marriage.

Chapter Five

Know what you want.

Most Christians doesn't know what they want when it comes to marriage.

Here's what I mean:

What kind of man or woman do you like?

A tall, short, slim, fat, average or whatever!

Most people think it doesn't matter; it matters a lot.

You have to know what you want and go for it. Marriage is a lifetime covenant relationship that is not meant to be broken according to **Malachi 2:16**

"For the LORD God of Israel says That He hates divorce... So, take your time and make a lasting choice. Marriage is for yourself enjoyment and not for your endurance. You're meant to have a heaven on Earth experience in your marriage According to **proverb 18:22**

Whoso finds a wife finds a good thing and obtains favor of the LORD.

You have the power of choice.

In **Deuteronomy 30:19 ...therefore choose life, that both thou and thy seed may live.**

Also, in **Mark 10:51 Jesus asked ..." what will thou that I should do unto thee?**

Another passage that establishes the fact god gives us the right to choose is **John 5:1.** Jesus went to the pool of Bethesda; there he saw a lot of sick folks. The bible recalls that when he came to a man that had infirmity for 38 years, He asked if he wanted to be healed.

God gives us the privilege to choose!

One of the best Right God gave mankind is the right to choose!

This is applicable to both men and women. Don't marry out of pity. Marry out of love, out of what you want.

Life is an adventure in choices, and every choice you make makes you.

Choice making is the act of selection, and selection indicates that there are alternatives or options.

Proverb 22:18 says he that finds... Marriage is by choice not by force.

Interestingly both the man and the woman are involved in making their choices.

Apart from Adam who woke up and found his wife, every other person in scripture had to find or to be found for. Abraham told his servant in **Genesis 24:4 But thou shalt go unto my country, and to my kindred, and take a wife unto my son Isaac.**

Your choice is to be made based on spiritual virtues, inner qualities not just physical appearance and materialism.

Marriage is a lifelong journey, don't make a permanent decision on a temporal feeling.

It's deeper than that! So, before you go ahead to choose your spouse understand that you have been empowered by God to make your choice.

You're given a free will to exercise power of choice. Even God respects the choices you make.

Despite that you have a power to choose, don't just choose carelessly because you have the power to choose, because next to salvation is your marriage choices.

If you are single here is a way to go about it:

pray, research, study, ask questions about the person before you choose. This is because your choices makes or mere you!

When Sampson chose Delilah over God's command, he suffered the consequences **Judges 16.**

So, if you expect a marital bliss, you need to choose wisely! To fulfill your glorious destiny, the choice of whom to marry should not be made in a haste. This is to avoid a lifetime of regret.

Before you make a choice of who to marry, consider the following:

- **Choose who you love.**

The love am talking about here is a deep affection for someone. This is one major requirement for a good marriage.

Romantic feelings and infatuation cannot equal to love.

Love is the glue that keeps relationship strong and solid in life. This Love is beyond feelings and attraction. This love is characterized in God according to **John 3:16**

Marriage is a lifelong relationship that needs a strong glue of love to cement it.

The Bible states in **1 Corinthians 13:8** that love never fails... So, until you are sure you love who you want to marry don't make the choice yet. Because love is what you need in the journey of marriage and if you are already married, you must consider to build your marriage on love.

You wonder how to know what this love is!

It is measurable according to **1 Corinthians 13:4-5**

Love is patient and kind. Love is not jealous or boastful or proud.

5 or rude. It does not demand its own way. It is not irritable, and it keeps no record of being wronged.

You can use these parameters to test it.

Love finds expression in thoughts, words and actions. When love is involved, it is always visible, you want to talk to each other, it shows off, you always want to please one another. You want him or her to Excel. And you're not ashamed of him or her, you're usually pleased to keep in touch with one another, that is a true love!

Someone who truly cares and love you, will always respect you privately and publicly.

- **You have to love your choice!**

In **Ephesians 5:33** the Bible said," **Nevertheless, let every one of you in particular so love his wife even as himself; and the wife see that she reverence her husband.**

So, you see it is not enough to marry someone you love you must also love who you chose.

If you're married and You wasn't aware of these, here is what the Bible said in **Ephesians 5:25 Husbands, love your wives, even as Christ also loved the church, and gave himself for it.**

God commanded that you love whosoever you married!

In marriage, falling in love is the beginning but staying in love is what really matters!

The moment you say yes, "I do", you're expected to give up all other options and cleave to your choice.

You must continue to love your spouse even when you don't feel like.

The unconditional type of love that helps spouses to forgive, respect, and serve one another; day in day, day out is what sustains a marriage.

Love does not insist on his rights!

Chapter Six

Success in Marriage.

No success story ever comes by accident. Success in marriage is not a product of luck or wish rather it occurs when both husband and wife intentionally accept responsibility and keep to their end of the deal.

To enjoy success in marriage therefore, you must nurture your marriage. And people who nurture their marriage reap one of the greatest treasures in life.

Now, you must understand that you're a major player in the success or failure of your marriage.

Research shows that one major secrets of success in marriage is that of showing respect.

What is respect?

Respect simply means, to honor, to reference and hold in a high esteem. It means a sense of worth and excellence of a person

Lack of respect in marriages are one of the major causes of crises in marriages and homes today.

It is what we all want and require in a relationship.

Wherever there is respect it cannot be hidden.

Showing respect is a necessity you should choose to be deliberate about, respect should be from the heart not just from the mouth.

Respect in marriages should be mutual, in other words, it should be two sided. In **1 peter 3:7**

Husbands, in the same way be considerate as you live with your wives, and treat them with respect as the weaker partner and as heirs with you of the gracious gift of life, so that nothing will hinder your prayers.

Also, in **Ephesians 5:33 ... and the wife must respect her husband.**

So, it is both ways!

Respect is a seed, the more of it you give the more of it you earn. It should not just be behind closed doors when you are alone! It should be in front of others and behind each other.

Respect in marriage begins referencing God and his word! A man or woman who respects God will naturally respect his or her spouse.

Respect to God is the first and foremost type of respect.

Couples that put God at the center of their marriage are usually successful, because you need God's help and strength.

Did you know that when you respect or obey any word of God concerning your marriage naturally you enjoy God's blessing?

When you obey God in your marriage you enjoy peace.

Let's look at what respect means to the husband in marriage.

No man or husband wants a disrespectful wife or woman.

So, respect the authority of your husband as the head of the home. Respect his knowledge, opinion and decision. Respect his unique quality and abilities that are in him.

To a wife, what does respect means!

To a wife, respect among other things means loving and cherishing her. Husbands, understand that your wife does not have to be a super model before she can receive regular sincere complement from you. Treat your wife as partner not as a property!

Don't treat her like slave, don't treat her as weakling, this will not help your marriage. Show unwavering commitment to your marital vows.

Now, you must understand what respect means, let's see where it starts from.

Respect begins from your thought because that's where every action originates.

If you think bitterness, evil, malice towards your spouse, it will one day manifest.

So, let good thought dominate your over your spouse.

Husband and wife respect each by not using foul languages. It can easily destroy. Show respect in your communication. Don't shout or belittle your spouse with your words.

Instead, encourage and appreciate your spouse, show kind gesture to him or her.

Chapter Seven

Pillars of success in marriage.

- **Trust.**

You must learn to trust your spouse or your partner! Trust here refers to having faith and belief in your spouse.

This gives peace of the mind, know what Your spouse is capable of doing, in order not be tracking them all of the time.

- **Patience.**

Men, please be patient with your wife, it's so vital. You have to learn to accommodate your wife. You know, women can be a bit unpredictable sometimes, they can be overcome with emotions sometimes, they can be overweighed with the weight of work.

Women are not as physically strong as men. When you expect a woman to always be on the go and on the move, she might seem to be lagging behind.

That's because of her physical constitution. Nevertheless, men have been encouraged to be patient with their wives.

Being patient in a relationship is absolutely necessary. And that's because, without tolerance, there is no true friendship that brings out the love in you. God has created us in a very unique way and each of us has our strengths and weaknesses.

Don't compare your spouses with other people. It brings desolation.

- **Kindness.**

Be kind to your spouse. In other words, be considerate! Reach out to your spouse, take care of him or her. **Ephesians 5**, the Bible tells the man to take care of his wife. Let her needs matter to you.

Let her burden becomes yours. Learn to pet your spouse, it's important. Don't make yourself so difficult for your wife or husband not to be able to feel free around.

Marriage is sweet believe me when you let all these have its place.

Men, be kind to your wife, help her and assist her

- **Appreciate each other all of the time.**

Appreciate each other All of the time.

 Naturally, people likes appreciation! People likes to be appreciated for what they did. I don't know about you but for me, I love it a lot.

Tell your spouse how beautiful and wonderful they are. When they dress, say to them "you look so beautiful, 'am glad I married you'" It doesn't cost much to do that but it makes and keep the marriage moving!

Even after intercourse, learn to appreciate your spouse. Don't be horrible because it doesn't suit marriage.

Learn to praise your spouse, just take out time and let your spouse know how awesome they have been to you!

- **Learn to say I am sorry.**

I am sorry is not weakness, it is strength in disguise! I Am sorry can quench a potential danger in a home, and not just that,

Also, learn how to talk your spouse, proverbs 15:1 says," A soft answer turns away wrath: but grievous words stir up anger." A soft word can bring healing to your spouse's soul when they are hurt badly! So, when you do things wrongly, humble yourself, even if you're the man. Say sorry to your wife! Likewise, the wife to your husband.

When you make mistakes confess to your spouse! Tell him or her 'you're sorry.

- **You must learn to forgive.**

The great man of God Billy Graham of blessed memory said, *"what makes a good marriage is two good forgivers."*

Human beings have weaknesses but the holy Spirit gives us strength to stand even where we have flaws.

Learn to forgive knowing that your spouse is a human, and he or she is not perfect.

In **Mark 10:8** the Bible said, **"and the two will become one flesh.'** So, they are no longer two, but one flesh.

Just like in the natural, now one slaps or beat up himself, or wrong himself. That's why God made them one because, everyone loves his or herself. So, only do to your spouse what you will do to yourself.

- **Make your home romantic.**

It's not all about sex, despite that sex has its great role to play.

There are ways to do this and they include:

- **Call each other sweet names.**

There are pet names, countless of them you can call your spouse! Don't let your marriage or relationship get cold.

I mean, who doesn't like to be called those names. It intoxicates!

- **Create out time to play.**

You can choose to play games if you're a game type or whatever activity you or your spouse may find interesting. These are ways to keep your marriage aglow!

You will realize that during these activities there's happiness, and joy.

- **Dress to entertain your spouse.**

This should be when you're alone. Let your spouse see you and be satisfied so that they won't have a cause to look outside! This creates desire. It makes you want more of your spouse!

If you don't know how to dress to entertain your spouse, learn it. This is especially for women; get those clothes you know that is entertaining; put them on and turn him on. This is very vital!

- **Prayer is the key**

There's a war to fight. You must understand that life is a Battle field and so is marriage. In **1 timothy 6:12** the Bible Said, **"fight a good fight of Faith...**

In today's world. We are faced with one of the greatest attacks in families. Unrest separation, devoice and unholy practices are ramparts in marriages.

Recently, there has been a general upward trend in divorce rate.

The truth is, the devil is actually behind the woes in marriages. Satan's mission has not yet changed which is usually to steal, kill and destroy According to **John 10:10**

And it's largely targeted at the home.

Please understand that you have an enemy. And your enemy is not your spouse but the devil.

Marriage is beautiful and therefore, the devil hangs around it to corrupt it.

In the first marriage in **Genesis 3:1-7** Satan didn't just try to make man disobey God; he also wants to bring division. The was why shame, secrecy, and accusation came after the eye open of Adam and Eve.

So, you must understand that you're at war with the devil who is against the success of your marriage.

You have to stay awake.

The good news is, this war is winnable in Christ.

The bible said in **revelation 12:11 and they overcame him by the blood of the lamb, and by the word of their testimony…**

You have to keep on pleading the blood of Jesus always whenever things keep on going in a way you don't understand it anymore. It's a language that put the devil in its place.

Conclusion

Marriage is much more like however you make your bed, so you shall lie on it. It is a responsibility demand-adventure, not just for the man alone or the woman alone. But for both of them.

You must carefully choose to work towards the success of your marriage. It's a call into responsibility. It's important to bear that in mind.

A lot of people just get into marriage and expects things to work by themselves. No, it doesn't work that way!

Building a successful home has a price. In **Luke 14:28** Jesus said**, "For which of you, intending to build a tower, sits not down first, and counts the cost, whether he have sufficient to finish it?**

Marriage indeed is a tower, and you must do just as Jesus said. You have to count the cost and also be willing to do it.

Marriage is not just theoretical, it's more of practical. You have to practice everything you have learned from this book and trust God for a blissful marital experience.

Anywhere you see a successful home just know it that it's two people who has agreed to love, pray, respect, Honor, appreciate, forgive and encourage each other.

There are lot of good things God has installed on marriage that you will reap as you choose to walk in the light of God's word.

Marriage isn't a wedding; it begins with a wedding. Just as every house has a door. Wedding is a door into marriage! Don't just prepare to make your wedding awesome without preparing adequately for your marriage.

Marriage tips for you

- Focus on your spouse's strengths rather than their weaknesses.

- Encourage rather than criticize.

- Pray for your spouse instead of gossiping about them.

- Focus on sustaining your relationship and cultivating an appreciation for one another daily.

- Be there for each other always.

- Don't be Selfish, it destroys home.

- Sacrifice your pride

- Overlook somethings just to let peace reign.

- Feel free to correct each other in a well respectable manner

- Learn to forgive each other.

- Provide sexual need to each other.
- Teach each other.
- Whatever you see in other.

Printed in Great Britain
by Amazon